CW01288147

GLASS PAPERWEIGHTS

Glass Paperweights

Patricia K McCawley

Charles Letts Books Limited

First published 1975
Revised edition 1982
by Charles Letts Books Limited
77 Borough Road, London SE1 1DW

Photographs: Michael Dyer Associates

© Charles Letts Books Limited

All rights reserved. No part of this publication may
be reproduced, stored in a retrieval system, or
transmitted, in any form or by any means, electronic,
mechanical, photocopying, recording or otherwise,
without prior permission of Charles Letts Books Limited

ISBN 0 85097 374 0

Printed and bound by Charles Letts (Scotland) Ltd

Contents

Introduction	7
Detail of canes	13
Detail of cutting	21
Story of Saint-Louis glassworks	24
Illustrations of Saint-Louis paperweights	27
Story of Baccarat glassworks	34
Illustrations of Baccarat paperweights	37
Story of Clichy glassworks	47
Illustrations of Clichy paperweights	48
The Gillinder family	52
Illustrations of Gillinder paperweights	53
Paul Ysart and family	54
Illustrations of Ysart paperweights	55
Story of Perthshire glassworks	57
Illustrations of Perthshire paperweights	58
Oriental paperweights	65
Illustrations of Chinese paperweights	66
Museums	69
Bibliography	71

Introduction

ALTHOUGH glass paperweights were collected before World War I, it was not until June 1952 that they were brought to the attention of a wider public when the first part of the late Mrs Applewhaite Abbott's large collection was sold at Sotheby's in London. By the time the three remaining parts had been sold, it was realized that an enormous variety of these colourful objects had been made between 1845 and 1860 – and subsequently they have become increasingly popular collector's items.

To appreciate the true fascination of a fine paperweight it must be handled. Because of the problems of reflection and transparency, photography can provide only a suggestion of the real beauty.

Legend had it that glass was discovered accidentally by a group of Phoenician sailors who built a bonfire on a beach and, having no stones to rest their cooking utensils on, used cakes of soda from their cargo. When they had eaten they were amazed to find that the soda had disappeared and in its place a hard shiny substance had appeared – the first glass made by man.

In a tomb of one of the old Pharaohs near Thebes, paintings on the walls show men blowing glass in very much the same way and with very much the same tools used today. Still preserved is a glass piece found in the tomb of Thutmore II who reigned about 1500 BC. Anyone who studies the old Egyptian mosaic glass beads will recognize the designs which reappeared hundreds of years later in the cane or florette patterns used in some of the early glass paperweights.

Many centuries later the art of glass making spread from Byzantium to Venice and Rome. In the twelfth century glass factories were so numerous in Venice that they became a city fire hazard and were moved to the Island of Murano, which continues to export fine glassware. There the secrets of glass making were guarded under penalty of death. Glass makers of those days ranked with the nobility: the daughter of a Count could marry a glass maker without losing caste. At Altare, the seat of the glass-makers' guild in the thirteenth century, glass workers were eventually hired out to other districts – much to the distress of Murano. As a result, the art spread to Bohemia, France, and England, and, centuries later, to the United States of America.

Frank Manheim, in his very readable book, *A Garland of Weights*, tells us that a member of an old family of Venetian glass artisans is credited with making the initial paperweight. He was Pietro Bigaglia. In May 1845, at the Austrian Industrial Fair in Vienna, Bigaglia displayed his hitherto unnoticed paperweights, one of the principal of which was 'a round-shaped millefiori [or thousand flowers] of highly transparent glass in which are embedded numerous small canes of all colours and forms assembled to look like a posy of flowers' (*Paperweights and Other Glass Curiosities*, E. M. Elville).

Attending the exhibition as an observer for the Paris Chamber of Commerce was Eugène Peligot, a professor at the *Conservatoire des Arts et Métiers*, and a renowned authority on glass. Impressed by Bigaglia's entry and, more important perhaps, quick to see a potential new product for the French glass industry which was not flourishing at the time, Peligot described the Italian's paperweights to friends in Paris and undoubtedly carried back with him to France examples of Bigaglia's innovation. The Frenchman's enthusiastic report proclaimed the birth of paperweights, and a contemporary account, *Les Press-Papiers Français de Cristal* (1948) by Roger Imbert and Yolande Amic, confirmed that 'millefiori paperweights were truly created in 1845 and were originated by Bigaglia of Venice'.

The most beautiful weights of all are the ones that were made in France by Baccarat, Clichy, and Saint-Louis, each factory having distinct characteristics in colouring, design, and – where the millefiori are concerned – type of cane (see illustrations pp 13–20). Subject weights, which contained a flower, vegetable, fruit, insect, or reptile, were distinctive, too. The star cutting on the base and around the dome also differed (see illustrations pp 21–23).

Sulphide weights which consisted of a ceramic medallion set in glass were started in the eighteenth century, and featured biblical figures and scenes, and also well known public figures such as Napoleon, Queen Victoria, and George Washington. They were made by many French firms including Baccarat, where they were set in clear glass or on a coloured background, Clichy, where a millefiori border was used, and, much later, by Saint-Louis. They were also made by the British firms of Apsley Pellatt (London) 1791–1863, John Ford and Company (Edinburgh) 1842–1897, William Kidd (London), and C. Osler (Birmingham).

To be able to appreciate paperweights fully it is necessary to know something of the raw materials, construction, and history in relation to the glass industry as a whole.

Glass, unlike many other familiar materials, never loses any of its original substance and weight, and is therefore an excellent medium for preserving artistic expression. The basic material is silica, which can be sand or quartz combined with an alkali – soda or lime; later, up to fifty per cent of lead oxide was added for strength and to increase the refractive index. Ravenscroft, the foremost English glass maker, discovered lead glass in the 1670s. By the late eighteenth century it was used extensively in France, where it was called crystal, just as in America today.

Lead glass takes a brilliant finish, and constitutes the foundation of all old paperweights and cut glass. It comes out of the furnace white hot, like iron, and the *metal*, as the molten glass is called, begins to change in its degree of ductility immediately. In the molten state it is extremely tough and elastic, and readily lends itself to ladling, pouring, casting, and stirring; in the viscous state it can be blown or rolled; and it remains plastic usually for about four or five minutes. It is generally transparent, but may be translucent or opaque.

All the raw materials placed in the melting pot are called *the batch*. Metallic oxides introduced into the batch can be used to produce various colours, although the result will depend upon the nature of the mixture and may be modified both by temperature and by the gases in the melting furnace. Copper oxide, for example, will produce green in a lead glass, and turquoise in a highly alkaline glass. The blue of cobalt, the chrome green or yellow of chromium, the violet of manganese, and the canary of uranium are all widely used. If oxide of copper is added to a mixture containing a strong reducing agent, a glass is produced which is colourless when it first comes from the crucible but which, when reheated, develops a rich crimson or ruby colour. Glass containing copper and gold behaves in much the same way, but with less intensity of the crimson effect. Cranberry red results from gold and copper mixed, oxblood from plain copper. Dark green can be produced from a mixture of copper scales and iron ore. Arsenic and antimony were used to secure the soft opaque enamel, sometimes called milk or opaque white, which we see on the overlay paperweights; also for the hard, opaque enamel which is found in the lacy 'set-ups' (see p 9) and *latticinio* (striped white glass) effects. Tin oxide and lead were used to provide a firm texture and a smooth surface to the mixture.

A furnace for melting glass materials is technically called a tank. When the metal is thoroughly heated, a scum or glass gall forms on the surface. This must be skimmed off. The process of refining continues by bringing the metal to a higher degree of heat in order to eliminate all bubbles. It is then allowed to cool to a point where it is no longer a liquid but a viscous mass which can be gathered on a blowpipe and formed.

Without attempting to cover the subject in all details, one highly important step in the process which should be mentioned is annealing, which is a systematic, gradual cooling to strengthen the product and make it resistant to the stresses and strains caused by changes of temperature. This takes up to twenty-four hours. Because of the many separate elements which enter into the complicated structure of a glass paperweight, it is essential that all parts be annealed uniformly. Otherwise, damage or destruction will result from cracking.

Fascinating as it is to handle a glass paperweight after completion, it is even more absorbing to watch the skilled glass makers creating the patterned base of the weight. In making a cane, for instance (see illustrations pp 13–20), the glass maker or *gaffer* will take a gather of coloured glass on to the end of a pontil rod and roll it into a cylindrical shape on a *marver* or iron table. He will add different layers of coloured glass depending on the effect he desires. When this is completed, another pontil rod is attached to the other end of the glass by his assistant, and the two men draw out the glass to a thin cylinder by walking away from each other, rotating the rod as they go, to keep a constant shape. The glass is then cut into thin cross sections, with an emery dipped in water.

Alternatively, differing shapes of canes can be achieved by thrusting a cylinder of hot glass into a shaped iron mould, and a similar process is repeated.

The cut sections of cane are arranged in metal rings into 'set-ups', cemented together with clear glass to form the patterned base of the weight.

Varieties other than millefiori require different techniques: for example, the petals, stems, and foliage in the flower and fruit weights are fashioned by means of tweezers held in each hand in front of a blowlamp. The flower or bouquet of flowers, butterfly, dragonfly, or reptile, when made, are picked up in the same way as the tray of canes.

To make the paperweight, one member of the team dips a pontil rod into the tank containing the molten glass which at this stage resembles a ball of sticky barley sugar. The rod is then held downwards in order to pick up the pattern from the tray, and this having been done, the rod is again dipped into the tank in order to collect more glass to form the dome above the pattern which then magnifies the canes. The dome is then shaped by rolling the pontil rod along a rail with one hand and creating the correct shape of the dome by holding the glass in a cup-shaped tool made of wood, which is kept in a pail of cold water to keep it cool after the intense heat of the glass that is being moulded each time a new paperweight is made. The paperweight is then squeezed at the base with a tool resembling a fire tongs, near where it is attached to the pontil rod, to enable it then to be tapped sharply so that it drops gently on some soft substance. It is then placed in the annealing oven to cool gradually and prevent cracking.

As each part of the process of making a paperweight is carried out entirely by hand, it can be assumed that those made in Victorian times, in France and Italy, were made in the same way as the modern French Baccarat and Saint-Louis, and Scottish paperweights being made today. The same pride and skill prevails.

Before and just after World War II it was only possible to collect antique paperweights, and as more and more people were competing in this field of collecting, the prices gradually became higher until only the wealthy could continue to acquire the finer and rarer pieces costing anything from £500 to £8,500. Paperweights had then entered the field of investment, like paintings and other fine art objects, where they remain today. Now, however, fine limited editions can also be collected at much less outlay, made by the few superior glass makers who take great pride in producing only the best in design and colour.

Unfortunately in recent years a number of inferior paperweights have appeared on the market, some of which require only the minimum of equipment such as a blow lamp and a small annealing oven which can be accommodated easily but which cannot, for instance, produce canes to form a frame around a flower bouquet in the centre, as seen in some of the illustrated examples.

To show up the colour and brilliance of well made paperweights, illumined cabinets or wall cases are ideal. For really extravagant display, recessed coffee tables can double as show cases.

For those contemplating starting a collection, however modest, they should read as many books on the subject as possible. The illustrations will show the great variety made, but even the coloured photographs cannot produce the three-dimensional effect necessary to do the weights justice. More important is to see as many examples as possible at auction houses such as Sotheby's, Christie's, and Phillips', in London; at Sotheby-Parke-Bernet in New York City; at the Auction House Hotel Druout in Paris; also in the stock of dealers who specialize in them. In this latter connection, for those with an eye to investment as well as pleasure, it is vital to seek the help and advice of a reputable dealer in order to avoid buying a weight of an erroneously accredited factory, or a weight that has been re-cut. The antique weights were cut very specifically by the three French factories, Baccarat, Saint-Louis, and Clichy.

Over the years many weights have been damaged, and while small chips and scratches can legitimately be removed from the surface with light and skilful polishing by lapidaries, the original shape must be retained. In some cases where they have suffered extensive bruising or chipping, unskilled glass cutters have removed the damage by cutting printies or facets (see, for example, diagrams on pp 21–23) which distort the shape and magnification, and destroy investment value. For the individual satisfaction to be gained, as well as from the investment point of view, it is better to buy one good paperweight a year than half a dozen inferior ones.

The following drawings should help those who enjoy wandering through small antique shops to recognize the specific canes or florettes and cutting made by the three French factories. Certain features distinctive to each factory are worth remembering: Saint-Louis produced less variety of cane than either Baccarat or Clichy, and sometimes included the initials 'SL' and the date; Baccarat frequently included the initial 'B' and a date between 1846 and 1849; rose canes were peculiar to Clichy, though they made no silhouette canes, and the star cutting on the base was quite different from the other two factories.

It is not possible to illustrate all types as the variety is endless. Apart from the millefiori weights, subject weights can be identified to some extent: for instance, Saint-Louis made weights with pansies, dahlias, clematis, camomile, fuschia, pears, cherries, apples, strawberries, and other common fruits, also a few snakes and salamanders; Baccarat made stylized flower weights of pansies, primroses, dahlias, roses, and buttercups, also butterflies and snakes; and Clichy's flowers, flat rather than upright, included pansies, dahlias, the occasional convolvulus, and ribboned bouquets or garlands – they also made a unique weight with caterpillars. One unidentified weight has potatoes and turnips in several colours, as the subject.

Saint-Louis flowers were often set against a coloured, latticinio, or *jasper* (mottled) ground; Baccarat used clear glass and Clichy clear glass or a moss or spiral ground. Clichy flowers were more delicate in colour than those of the other two factories: its pansy, for instance, resembled a violet or wild pansy in pale mauve and pale yellow or cream, while the two large upper leaves of the Baccarat pansy were often rich plum, the rest a mustard yellow; the Saint-Louis variety was also rich coloured but smaller than the Baccarat. Of the snakes made by the French factories, Saint-Louis's were coiled on a latticinio ground, while Baccarat's ground resembled rock.

A little-known French factory, Cristallerie de Pantin, produced beautiful flowers and fruit, sometimes set on an opaque white ground. Also the American New England Glass factory made flowers – dahlia, pansy, poinsettia – often on latticinio cushions, and groups of pears also on latticinio, though their main products were millefiori weights and overlays. Modern versions of snakes are made by one or two American lamp workers, and by Paul Ysart in Scotland. Weights of ducks or swans on a pond were made by Baccarat or Saint-Louis (no-one seems quite certain), and a small number of modern ones were made by Paul Ysart and Perthshire Paperweights.

The (English) Whitefriars Glass Company made paperweights with concentric circles of canes set in clear glass between 1848 and 1853, and started again in 1953 when they made a paperweight to commemorate the Coronation of Queen Elizabeth II. This particular weight had a large central cane with 'E II R 1953'. This factory continues to make weights of this type without a special central motif. George Bacchus & Son, Birmingham, made some fine concentric and composite cane weights, around 1850. Other English firms that produced paperweights include Rice, Harris and Co, Islington; Glass Works, Birmingham; W H B and J Richardson of Wordsley, Stourbridge; Thomas Hawkes and Co, Dudley; and J G Green, London.

The US firms that produced paperweights, besides the New England Glass Company, include: Sandwich Glass Works, Cape Cod, whose products, mostly millefiori and flower weights, are similar to those of the New England factory; South Ferry Glass Works, Brooklyn, New York, who produced bouquet weights; The Mount Washington Glass Works, New Bedford, who made flower and strawberry weights; Millville Works, New Jersey, who are famous for the Millville rose, which is upright, and often provided with a pedestal; and, today, Charles Kaziun, who makes flower weights with a signature cane 'K', a pedestal, and often inserts gilt dragonflies, butterflies, and bees.

In an endeavour to show the variety of antique and the finer modern paperweights, short histories of the factories that created them follow, with illustrated examples from each.

Canes

Baccarat

1 **Silhouette.** Usually in black or white, of a

(a) dog, (b) cockerel, (c) deer, (d) horse, (e) monkey, (f) swan, (g) squirrel, (h) goat, (i) elephant, (j) pigeon, (k) pelican, (l) butterfly, (m) hunter with rifle, (n) kangaroo, (o) flower, and (p) clown

these set in white or blue in pastry mould cane edged with different colours, such as turquoise, red, yellow, mauve, green, etc. or in hollow canes lined in different colours.

2 **Star-dust.** Composed of one central rod surrounded by six rods of star shape in white with red centres. Canes with as many as 19 of these are to be seen. Other types of star shaped rods are seen in white, and sometimes within an outer casing of coral pink, green or mauve, and are sometimes set within a hollow tube. These star shapes are also found outlined in colour in a solid white cane.

3 **Arrowhead.** Looks rather like a little flowerhead,

(a) sometimes with central white rod with red star outline, surrounded by eight white 'petals' with dark blue arrow pointing towards centre, set in red, and

(b) surrounding whorls.

BACCARAT

1(a)    1(b)    1(c)

The arrows are also found in green and red, set in different colours. This cane also appears as a stylized 'flower' with honeycomb centre in a bouquet weight, much larger in size, and as a centre of single flowers.

4 Trefoil. Seven or more hollow white rods with red trefoil centres joined together to form a cane. Also incorporated in other canes with whorls, in other colours.

5 Quatrefoil. Usually seen as four hollow white rods with turquoise quadrifoil centres, but also turquoise within white with outer casing of coral pink or other colour.

BACCARAT

1(d)

1(e)

1(f)

1(g)

1(h)

1(i)

1(j)

1(k)

1(l)

6 Honeycomb. In cream or white, seen as a separate cane in a millefiori weight and often as the centre of a flowerhead.

7 Whorl. Often forming the centre of a star-dust cane, in green, pink, blue or yellow. Sometimes found in a cane composed of one central whorl surrounded by nine others, each of a different colour.

8 Shamrock. Mostly seen in an inner circle to a cane, but occasionally one or two are found beneath a silhouette, or otherwise included in a cane.

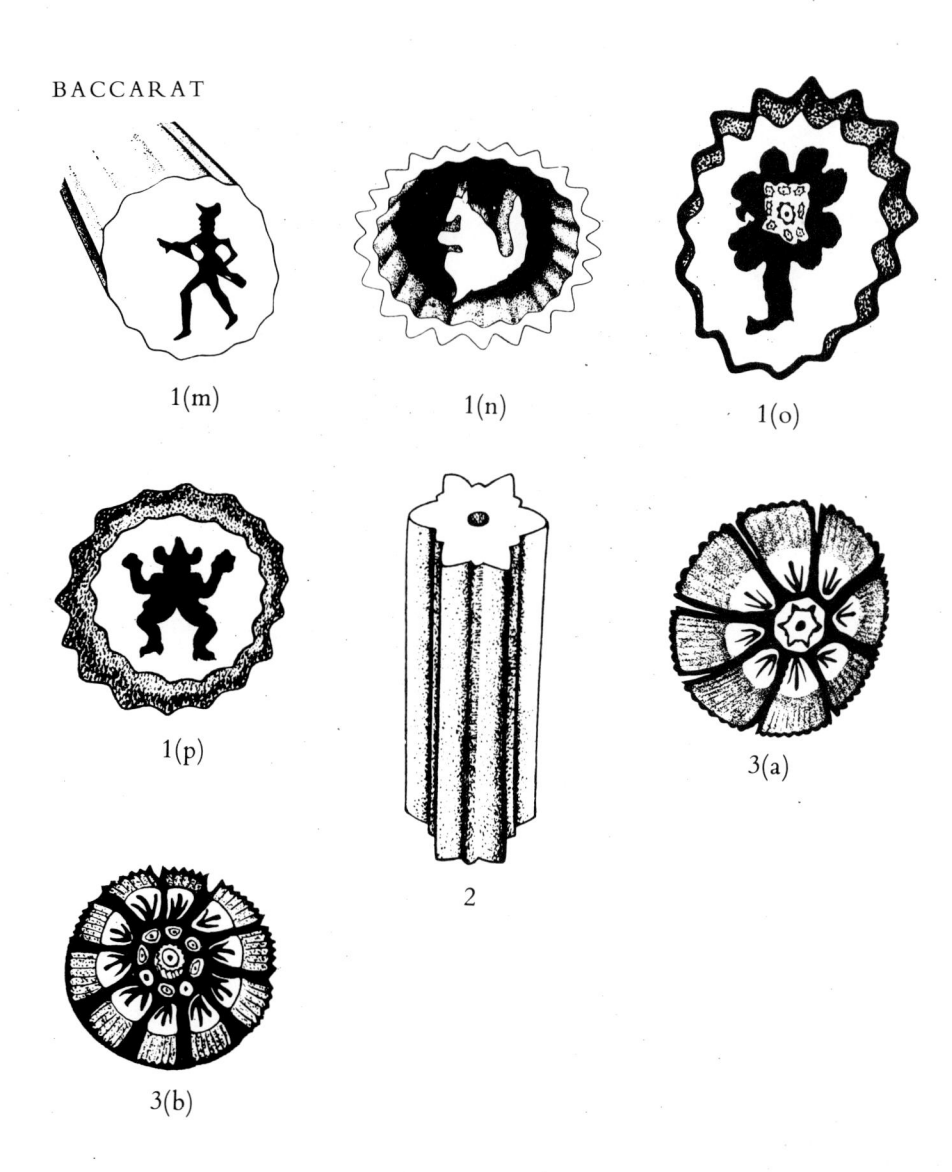

BACCARAT

1(m)

1(n)

1(o)

1(p)

2

3(a)

3(b)

BACCARAT

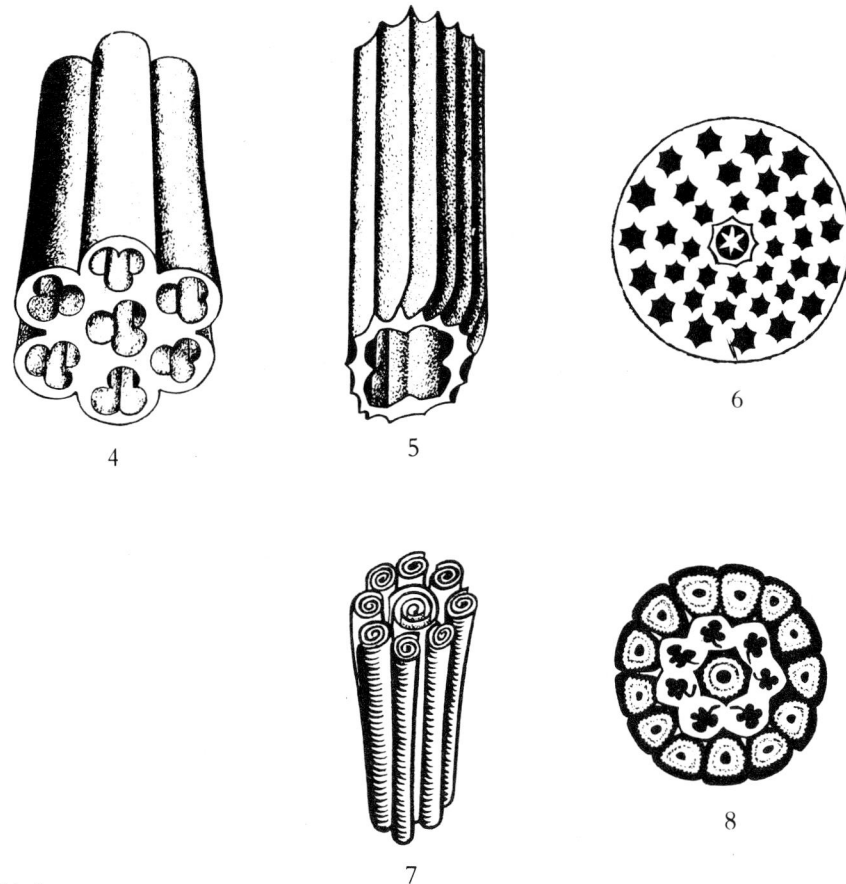

          4   5   6

                             7   8

Clichy

9 Rose. Composed of a multitude of leaflets packed together, the most common and typical are in pink within an outer row of green leaflets, but also found in all white, sometimes with pink outer leaflet, all yellow, and mauve with white outer leaflet.

10 Pastry Mould. This appears in various shapes and colours with white, the centres with stamens or silhouettes.

11 Letter 'C'. Found in black, blue, green or red, set in white, sometimes within a circle of whorls and/or star-dust rods. Although this 'signature' is not essential to prove a paperweight was made by this factory, it is an added attraction.

12 Word 'Clichy'. This is extremely rare and the letters – sometimes appearing as 'CL', 'ICHY', or 'CHY' – are seen in single white rods, perhaps with a whorl or other rod, surrounding a pastry mould rod. It is also seen written amidst millefiori canes in a weight or vase. As with No. 11 this adds interest and value to a paperweight.

13 Moss. Composed of translucent green rods with white starlets packed together to resemble moss.

14 Stars. Tiny pure white rods, some solid and some with round hollow centres as many as 24 forming a cane; also surrounding a coloured whorl, and sometimes with tiny red centre within a hollow tube lined with a different colour.

15 Whorl. Similar to Baccarat, either centrally in a cane or in a circle within a cane, the outer section of which can be within a circle of other typical Clichy rods or a pastry mould of pink, mauve, green, etc. lined with white. These whorls are green, rose-pink, all white, or white with red centres, mauve or turquoise.

16 Hollow tube. This sometimes forms the centre, white lined with a colour, set within a pastry mould; sometimes with crimped edges similar to those of Saint-Louis but very much smaller.

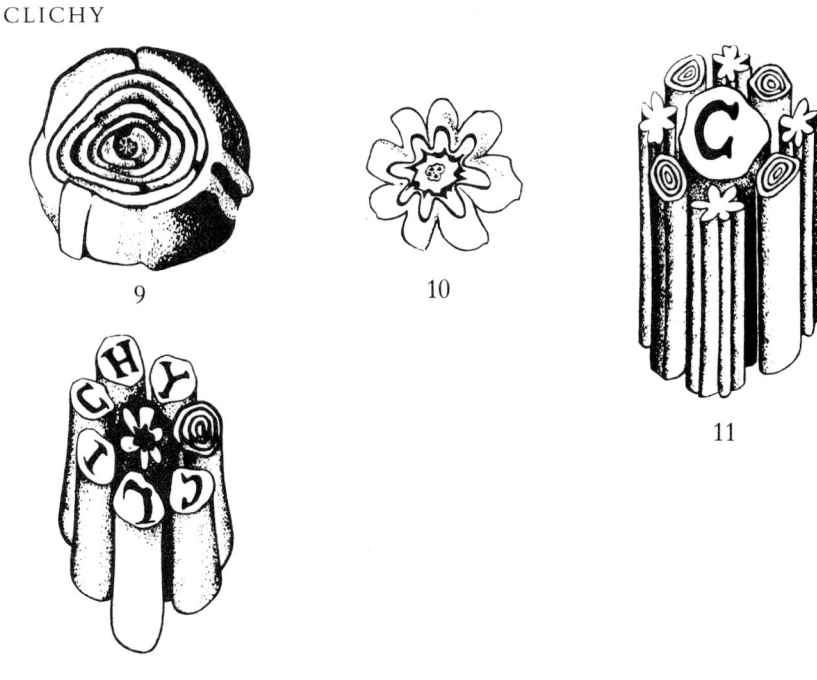

CLICHY

9

10

11

12

CLICHY

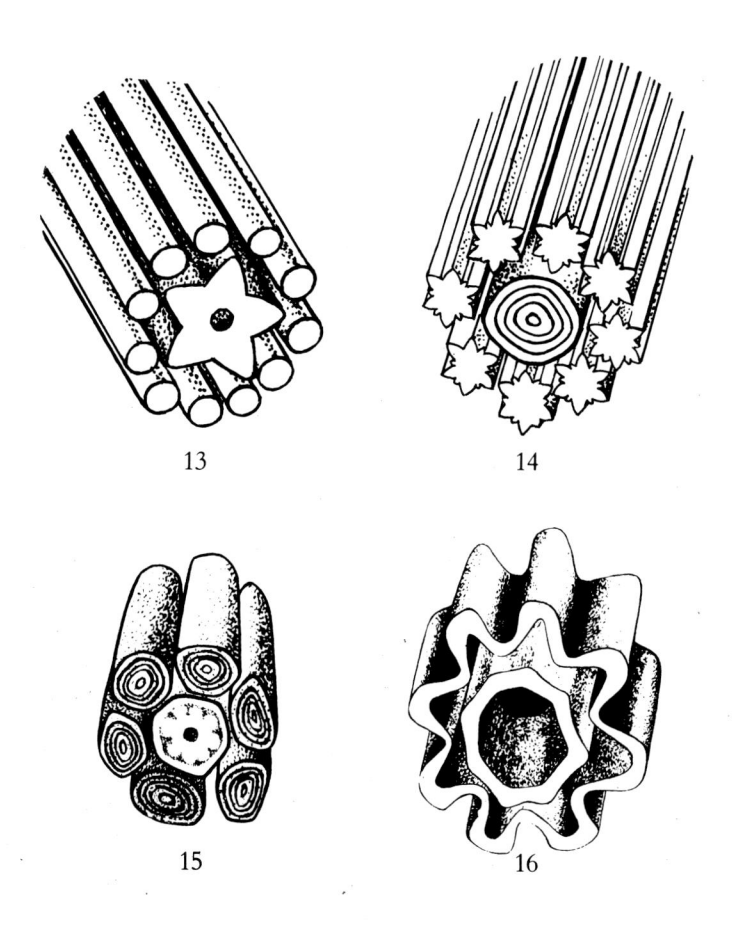

13

14

15

16

Saint-Louis

17 Silhouette. Usually in black or white of a

   (a) camel, (b) one dancing figure, (c) two dancing figures, (d) dog,
   (e) horse, (f) bird, (g) dancing devils, and (h) devil (two varieties)

the black silhouettes set in solid white with crimped edge, the white set in hollow tube with similar edge, lined with different colours.

18 Hollow Tube. This is mostly in two colours, with crimped edge, the outside differing from the lining. Found in blue and yellow, pink and white, blue and white, amber and blue, green and white, two shades of pink, and red and white. Also three-coloured, white with pink lining, with rod of blue in centre (extremely rare). Another striking type occurs in a white hollow lined with a colour such as green, with outer frill of white lined with a colour such as pink.

19 Arrowhead. Although this is rarely seen in Saint-Louis weights, it does exist and a circle of them in a dated millefiori paperweight is recorded. There are seven outer sections to the cane, the black arrow pointing towards the centre set in solid white within pink outer casing, the central section composed of a quadrifoil in pink and white. It has also been seen in a central rod in a cane, the arrows in red set in solid white within an outer casing of blue, pointing both inwards and outwards.

20 Initials 'SL'. In black set in a solid white cane.

21 Star. White with coloured hollow or solid centres set within a frill of white or blue; also seen within hollow tube with crimped edge.

SAINT-LOUIS

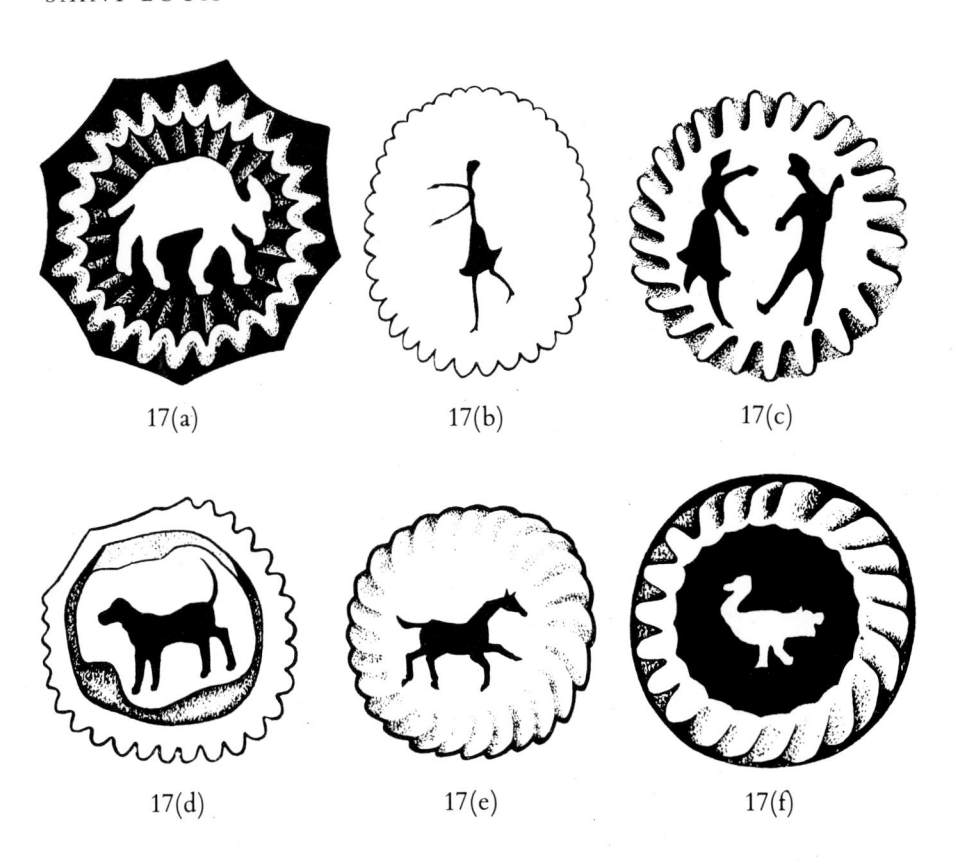

17(a)

17(b)

17(c)

17(d)

17(e)

17(f)

SAINT-LOUIS

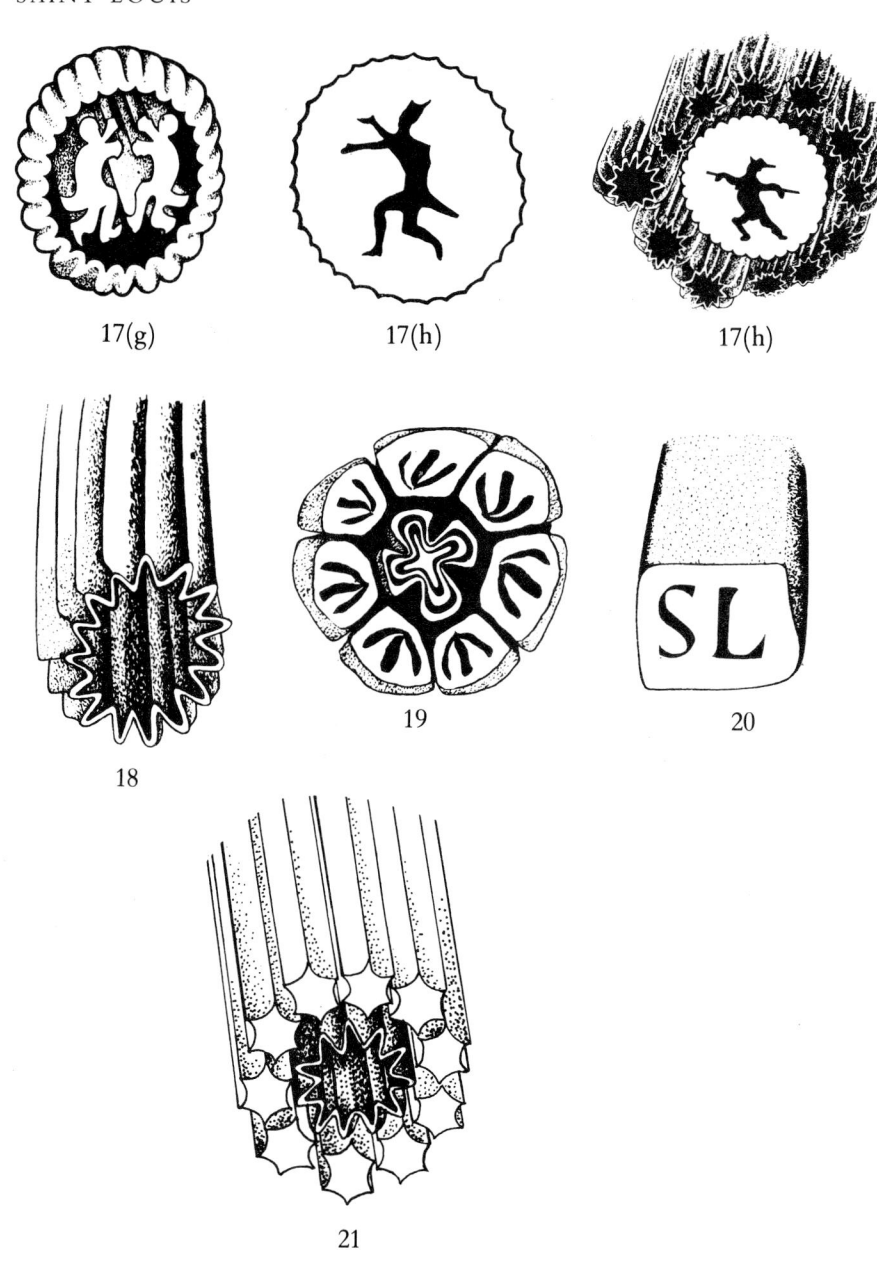

17(g)   17(h)   17(h)

18   19   20

21

Cutting

Baccarat

1. Flash (or translucent) overlay type, with top and six side printies and broad flutes at base.

2. Opaque double overlay with top and five or six side printies.

3. Top printy and hexagonal diamond cutting down to base.

4. Top printy and numerous small, medium and large side printies down to base.

5. Top and six side printies.

6. Top and six side printies, with deep star cutting across base.

7. Opaque double overlay, with top and six side printies and numerous small printies round base.

8. Large top printy with diamond cutting down to pedestal base.

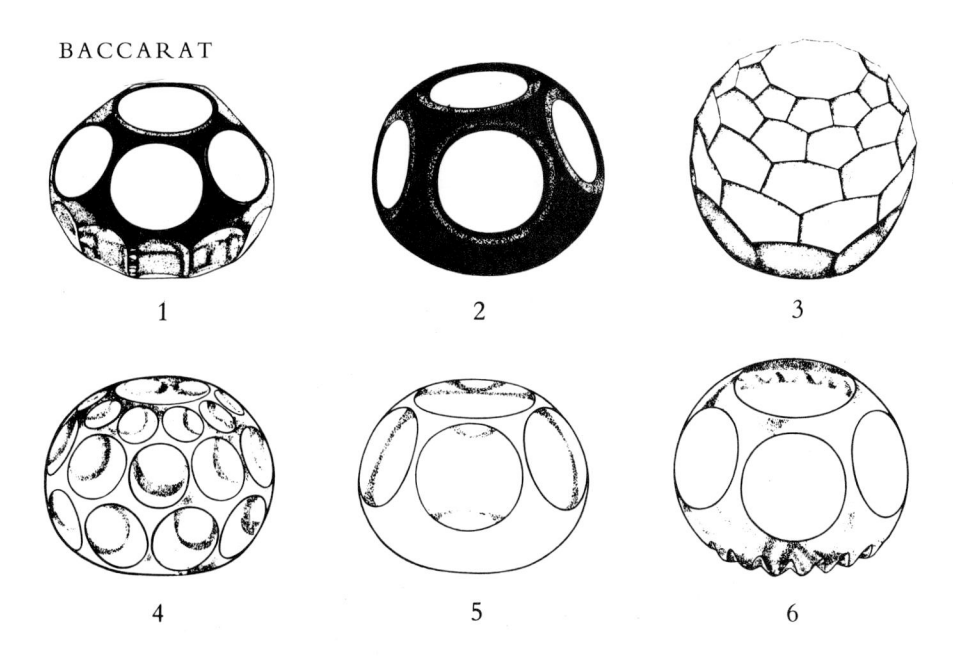

BACCARAT

BACCARAT

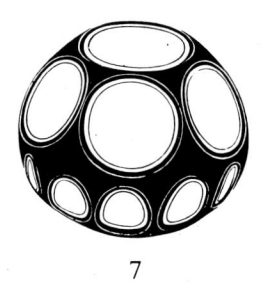

7

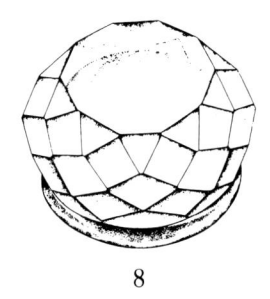

8

Clichy

9 Top printy, with five side printies divided by flutes.

10 Type 1. Opaque double overlay with flat top, five side printies and star cutting on base.

10 Type 2. Opaque double overlay with flat top, five side printies and strawberry cutting on base.

CLICHY

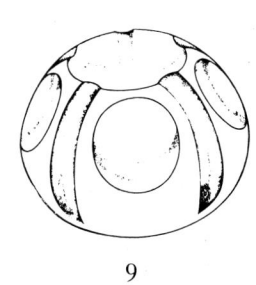

9

10 (type 1)

10 (type 2)

22

Saint-Louis

11 Encased double overlay, with internal top and six side printies encased in clear glass.

12 Top printy with graduated facets down to base.

13 Honeycomb facets on the top, with side printies, and strawberry cutting across base.

14 Small printies on the top, with side printies, and strawberry cutting across base.

15 Top printy with diamond facets down to base.

16 Honeycomb facets all over.

SAINT-LOUIS

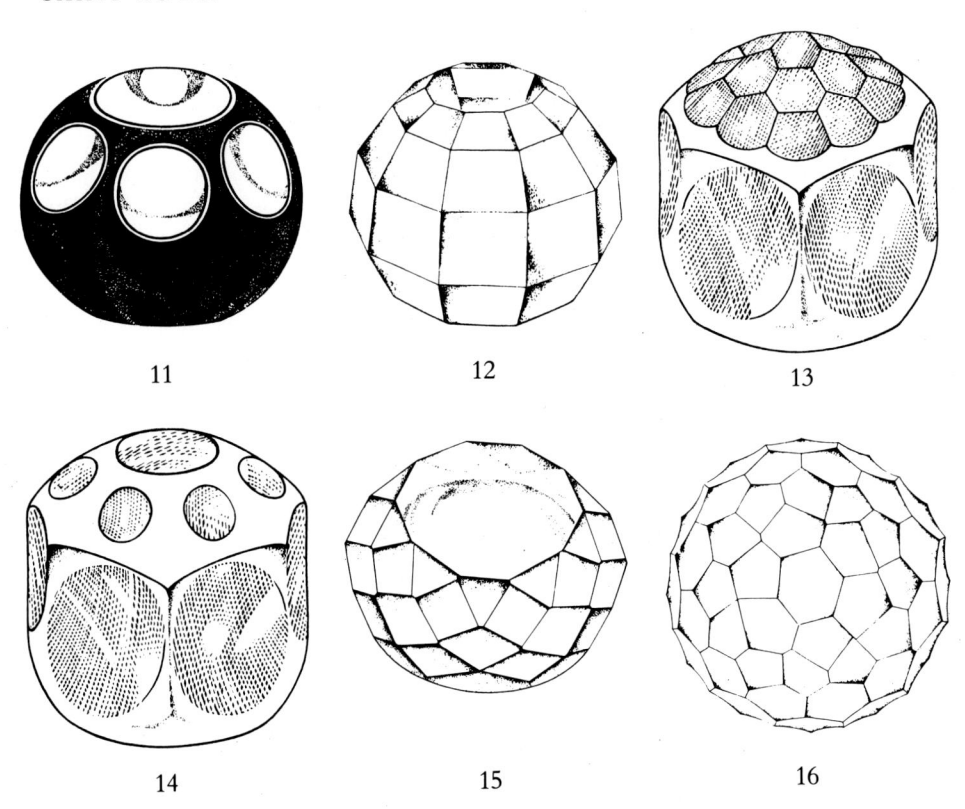

The Compagnie des Cristalleries de Saint-Louis

A VERY OLD factory devoted for nearly four hundred years to the same industry, Saint-Louis is a national institution. Work has altered very little in the village of Lorraine where the factory is based: men are glass makers or cutters from father to son. If the tools are different, the love of the handicraft remains the same. Only tastes have changed.

The glass industry was known to Lorraine many centuries ago as can be seen from the Gallo-Roman remains near Sarrebourg and the creation of the first glass factories before the sixteenth century. In 1469 the glass workers' charter of the Duke of Lorraine granted special privileges to this industry which was able, as early as the fifteenth century, to set up various factories in the district of Bitche in the far eastern part of the Moselle. All the necessary raw materials were available in the area: wood in the forests – this was at the time the only fuel in use; the sand to be found in the soil; the soda in the salt mines of the Haute-Sarre; and the potash extracted from fern ashes. It was in 1586 that first mention was made of the glassworks of Munsthal. Unfortunately its prosperity was short-lived on account of the devastations caused by the wars during the seventeenth century and particularly the Thirty Years War from 1618–48.

Shortly after Lorraine was annexed by France in 1766, two barristers, René François Jolly and Pierre Etienne Olliver, obtained from Louis XV certain rights over Munsthal with the obligation of building a glass factory there. They were also given some 8,000 acres of the forest of Bitche to provide the wood for heating the furnaces. An area of this extent was necessary if deforestation was to be avoided. The decree also granted the title of *Verrerie Royale de Saint-Louis* to the new glass factory, and scarcely one year later, three years after the establishment of the Baccarat factory, drinking ware of the first quality was being produced.

It was in 1780 that the great event occurred: the Comte de Beaufort, director of the factory, produced crystal for the first time. This achievement was officially recognized by the Royal Academy of Science, meeting on 12 January 1782, when Cassini, Lalande, Condorcet, Monge, Laplace, Lamarch, Daubenton, and Lavoisier, among other celebrities, were present. Various drinking glasses from the factory were examined and compared with objects in English crystal. The new French crystal and the English were found to be identical, both in clarity and specific weight, and also in the possibility of use in achromatic lenses. By a decree of 25 May 1784, the State Council recognized officially that 'the French crystal is as well manufactured as that of the British' and declared that it should be useful both to commerce and the State in saving a considerable amount of foreign currency.

This discovery was of course responsible for the great prosperity of Saint-Louis. Baron de Dietrich of the Royal Academy of Science wrote of the 'four glass melting furnaces of which three were in constant use, twelve furnaces for making sheet and flat glass of which ten were in constant use, thirteen for drying the wood used to melt the glass, one furnace for burning the refractory clay, a crushing shop, a pottery shop, and several other workrooms and shops'. The factory became the centre of a community. To the houses of the owners, directors, employees, and the buildings in which the workers were housed – accounting for a total of 637 people – were added a church, school, and surgery.

In 1785, to avoid workers being enticed away, the State Council issued a decree forbidding a worker to leave the area without having obtained permission. According to Dietrich, in 1788 Saint-Louis was one of the best factories in the kingdom, with a yearly turnover of 240,000 pounds.

From 1791–95 Saint-Louis was managed by Aimé Gabriel d'Artigues who later bought the Belgium factory of Vonêche, near Liège, in 1802. In 1816, as a result of the export barriers introduced by the treaty of Vienna, d'Artigues foresaw the closing of the French market to his Belgian glass exports and, accordingly, bought the factory in Sainte-Anne at Baccarat, France, which became a crystal factory in 1819 (see p 35).

In 1829 Seiler Walter & Co, the owners of Saint-Louis since 1809, became a public company under the name *Compagnie des Verreries et Cristalleries de Saint-Louis*, with a capital of 1,200,000 francs divided into 120 shares. This was the beginning of a second era of great prosperity. As early as 1820 Saint-Louis was the first crystal factory to use pressure moulding, to have moulded objects in crystal with sharp edges which could not be obtained by ordinary blowing methods.

In 1831 the two big crystal factories of the East, Saint-Louis and Baccarat, were more closely united. Their directors, Seiler and Goddard, often consulted each other and grouped together for the sale of their products, owning a common warehouse in Paris in the rue de Paradis from 1831–57.

In 1832 Saint-Louis and Baccarat bought the crystal works of Saint-Cloud which had been transferred to Mont-Cenis near the Creusot. (They were eventually to sell out in 1937 to the Schneider Co.) Thus Saint-Louis was for a certain length of time joint owner of what was to become the *Creusot*. This was the period during which paperweights and sulphides (see p 8) were popular, later to become very expensive: for example, in 1957 a paperweight in the collection of Maurice Lindon, a green encased overlay, was sold for £1,250; and another in the same collection, a yellow encased overlay was sold for

£2,700 – the only weight with yellow overlay discovered to date.

It was also at this time that crystal encased with several different colours came into being, together with opalines which were first made in 1844. Overall, the period was remarkable for its study of shape and colour, and for the improvement of quality and the purification of raw materials. It was also the golden age for the tariff protection of crystal.

During the period 1860–95 the quality of the products was improved by replacing wood firing with coal firing. The last wood-fired furnace was extinguished in 1866, and the first Siemens furnace with regenerators fired by coal gas was put into operation in 1863. In between, a few Boetius coal-fired furnaces were used from 1855–1864. During this same period the directors abolished work on Sundays, instituted piece work, and provided a common fund for retirement and sickness.

From 1860 to 1867 Saint-Louis had workshops in Paris, employing 150 workers specialized in painting, decorating, and gilt-bronze mounting. French crystal was world-famed for its choice of colours and shapes: clear crystal, plain, moulded, coloured, cut, decorated or engraved. In 1860 the method of acid engraving was adapted for use in frosting and engraving crystal.

However, from 1850 Saint-Louis seem to have stopped manufacture of paperweights until 1967 when one was made in limited edition with sulphide portrait of Saint-Louis to commemorate the bi-centenary of the founding of the factory (see p 31). This also marked the renewal of glass-paperweight making, both floral and millefiori – at prices comparable to those made in the nineteenth century.

The annual turnover of Saint-Louis places it among the great crystal factories of the world.

Antique Saint-Louis mushroom of canes in concentric circles with date SL 1848 contained in salmon pink basket within royal blue and white twist ring. Star cutting on base. $2\frac{3}{4}''$ diameter

Antique Saint-Louis mushroom of canes in concentric circles contained in ochre basket, within salmon pink and white twist ring. Star cutting on base. $2\frac{3}{4}''$ diameter. *Circa* 1845–60

27

Saint-Louis concentric millefiori with dancing figures and date SL 1848. 3″ diameter

Saint-Louis mixed fruit in latticinio basket. 2½" diameter. *Circa* 1845–60

Saint-Louis turnips in latticinio basket. 2½" diameter. *Circa* 1845–60

29

Antique Saint-Louis upstanding posy of flowers, florettes, and green foliage within white double twist ring, cut with top printy and rows of facet cutting. $2\frac{3}{4}''$ diameter. *Circa* 1845–60

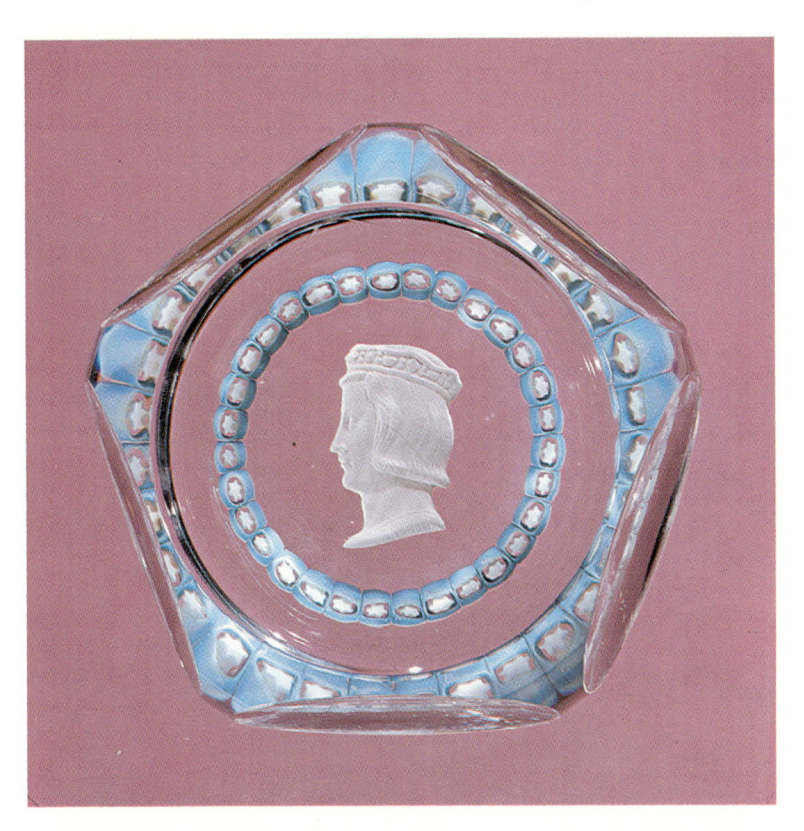

Modern Saint-Louis sulphide of Saint-Louis within circle of canes, with top and side printy cutting. Made to commemorate the bicentenary of Saint-Louis. Dated on reverse of portrait SL 1767–1967. $2\frac{3}{4}''$ diameter

Modern Saint-Louis bouquet of flowers, foliage, and stalk, set in opaque white cushion, with top and side printies. Date cane SL 1971 in centre of flower. $2\frac{3}{4}''$ diameter

Modern Saint-Louis teal and white double overlay with canes in star-shaped pattern set in translucent blue cushion, but with top and side printies. Date cane SL 1971 in centre. $2\frac{3}{4}''$ diameter

Modern Saint-Louis white auricula with yellow centre cane dated SL 1973, bud, foliage, and stalk set in opaque coral pink cushion. 3″ diameter

Modern Saint-Louis marbrie of teal blue and white festoons, with central date cane SL 1971. 3″ diameter

The Compagnie des Cristalleries de Baccarat

In 1764 the Bishop of Metz, Montmorency-Laval, owned land in the southern part of Lorraine. The establishment of a wood-burning glassworks seemed to the Bishop the best way of putting his vast forests to profitable use. Accordingly he sent a petition to King Louis XV pointing out that 'France produces no art glass, and this is why Bohemian glassware is imported in such large quantities, causing an enormous outflow of funds at a time when the kingdom has such great need of them to recover from the terrible Seven Years' War'. The petition also emphasized the poverty of the woodcutters, unemployed since 1760. His arguments were all well founded, and the request was granted by the King and his council at Fontainebleau on 16 October 1764.

Several months later, the Parliament of Metz registered the company. The number of furnaces that could operate simultaneously was limited to three. A suitable site had to be found for the factory, to be located close to the transportation route for the fuel, namely the Meurthe River on which the wood was floated, and it was also logical to choose a well populated village from which young men could be recruited for training as skilled craftsmen. The village of Baccarat was then situated on the left bank of the Meurthe, and the Bishop decided to build the glassworks on some vacant land across from it on the right bank of the river. During the first few years he engaged a technician named Antoine Renaut to run the factory.

The business grew rapidly, as shown by the consumption of raw materials during the years 1766 to 1769: 600 tons of sand, 300 tons of rock salt, and 40 tons of ashes. Fuel consisted solely of wood and amounted to 6,400 cords per year (a cord being 128 cubic feet), according to a report of 1791 for the district of Luneville. The shipping of such a large quantity of wood could only be done by floating it, and this necessitated digging a canal from the Meurthe which ran the entire length of the glassworks.

At the same time, lodgings for the workers were constructed. One account of the time mentions dwellings for seventy families. All these dwellings were built within the confines of the factory. At that time the fusion point of all the elements for glass was very unpredictable and depended on a number of factors such as the general condition of the wood and atmospheric conditions. When the molten glass was just right a bell was rung to summon the artisans. The working hours of necessity varied each day, so it was imperative that the workers lived near by.

On 12 December 1806 the Company was sold at auction and acquired by an industrious merchant from Verdun, Lippmann-Lippmann. After two years he took on an associate named Duroux. However, orders became so rare, in a country half ruined by the Napoleonic Wars, that it became necessary in 1811 to shut down two furnaces and keep only 70 workers out of a total of 400.

For a few years the business limped along. The cost of fuel was prohibitive and manpower was reduced to a bare minimum by military conscription. Finally, on 15 May 1816 the factory was bought for 2,845 ounces of fine gold by Monsieur d'Artigues, the owner of the crystal factory of Vonêche in Belgium (see p 25), who had found himself, after the peace treaties of 1815, the head of a Belgian industry unable to export its products to France because of strict tariff regulations. He, therefore, asked King Louis XVIII to allow him an exemption from these tariffs. The King agreed on condition that within two years the Belgian would build a factory in France which would produce at least 500 tons of crystal annually. In return, d'Artigues obtained permission to bring in each year 500 tons of unfinished crystal from Belgium which would be cut and decorated in France.

On 9 April 1817, after much difficulty, he received the King's permission to install his crystal factory at the glassworks of Baccarat. He was allowed to have four furnaces, each with twelve open melting pots. The firm's name then became *Verrerie de Vonêche à Baccarat*. D'Artigues was also allowed to build a factory near by for making lead oxide which he was to use in great quantities in the making of glass. The factory employed 300 workers compared with 60 in 1814, and the production of anything other than lead crystal was discontinued. In addition a large cutting workshop was established.

In 1823 d'Artigues sold the crystal works for 396,000 francs to three of his associates, Pierre-Antoine Godard, Lescuyer, and M Lolot. The *Compagnie des Cristalleries de Baccarat* emerged the following year as the result of this purchase.

Godard realized that the key to success for Baccarat would always be the perfection of its products. He imported his potash from America. The selection of lead oxide and the finest sand was also a constant preoccupation. It was not enough to have the finest materials: Godard felt they had to be used by craftsmen who would, with each succeeding generation, and with better and better training, become the finest crystal makers in the world.

The Bohemian glass industry became more and more of a serious competitor of Baccarat as it was the only industry in 1835 to make coloured glassware. The process was kept secret, and attracted the attention of scientific circles everywhere. In 1838 the *Société d'Encouragement* in France offered a reward of 8,000 francs to anyone who could discover the colouring process. The mystery was finally solved – by an executive of Baccarat, Monsieur de Fontenay, who was to become Assistant Manager of Baccarat in 1841 – and the Bohemian colouring process was duplicated.

In 1846 the factory made a new type of article, the millefiori paperweight.

The fine flower-like canes were later incorporated into ornamental pieces and even stemware. Towards 1850 the exhaustion of the wood supply threatened the company: industry was developing in Lorraine with breweries, tile, salt, and iron works consuming more and more wood. Emile Godard and Fontenay sought first to control the temperature of the furnaces by the methodical drying of wood cut into equal lengths, so that the fusing of the crystal would always be regular.

Next began the search for coal. Several unsuccessful excavations were made in the area. The factory was finally forced to buy a large forest near by until such time as the railroad, then under construction, could bring in coal. The first efforts at heating with coal gas were begun in 1853 and were finally successful in 1856. The costs were terribly high by comparison with those of foreign competition which was still using wood acquired at reasonable prices.

The sulphide and millefiori paperweights, perfected in 1848, were in demand until about 1880, then disappeared from popular view for 70 years. Revived in 1952, the sulphides seem to be as popular among collectors as the older ones. The millefiori, for which the technique was not rediscovered by Baccarat's chief engineer until 1958, are even more rare and appreciated, especially in the United States.

The Cristalleries de Baccarat carried the prestige of France beyond its borders over many years, its success due, in part at least, to its management and the generations of craftsmen and workers that have remained united by loyalty to their company. The first owners of the Company were real pioneers in the realm of social welfare. From the start, dwellings for the workers were built round the factory. In 1827 the Company had a doctor in residence and a school for boys. In 1831 a savings bank was created for the benefit of the employees, and a disability fund was started in 1835, a century before Social Security and family benefits became law under the Pierre Laval Government. This set of social institutions, unique in history, won for Baccarat the grand prize at the *Exposition Sociale* in Paris in 1889. The Company is just as proud of this award as it is of all its gold medals and grand prizes won over two centuries in all the national and international exhibitions and fairs. After surviving four foreign invasions in less than two centuries (1815, 1870, 1914, 1940), and three revolutions (1789, 1830, and 1848), Baccarat became practically the only company which passed through the period of great social upheavals of 1936 and 1968 without a factory strike. At the present time it makes about three hundred paperweights a year.

Antique Baccarat royal blue and white primrose with bud with honeycomb centre, foliage, and stalk, within circle of canes. Cut with top and side printies. Star cutting on base. 3″ diameter. *Circa* 1845–60

Antique Baccarat red and white primrose and bud with star-dust centre, foliage and stalk, within circle of canes. Star cutting on base. 2½″ diameter. *Circa* 1845–60

Antique Baccarat blue and white wheatflower, foliage, and stalk. 2½″ diameter. *Circa* 1845–60

Antique Baccarat white pom-pom dahlia with yellow stamens, bud, foliage, and stalk, within circle of canes. Star cutting on base. 3″ diameter. *Circa* 1845–60

Antique Baccarat coral pink pom-pom dahlia, bud, foliage, and stalk within circle of canes. Deep star cutting across base. 3″ diameter. *Circa* 1845–60

39

Antique Baccarat gentian blue dahlia with star-dust centre, bud, foliage, and stalk, within circle of canes set in white latticinio. 3″ diameter. *Circa* 1845–60

Antique Baccarat bouquet of white dahlia with honeycomb centre, red and white primrose with star-dust centre, and forget-me-not with star-dust centres, foliage, and stalks. Star cutting on base. 3″ diameter. *Circa* 1845–60

Baccarat white carpet with cross-shaped garland. $3\frac{1}{4}''$ diameter. *Circa* 1845–60

Antique Baccarat blue and white double overlay with small mushroom within made of concentric circles of canes in white basket. Cut with top and side printies. Star cutting on base. 3″ diameter. *Circa* 1845–60

Antique Baccarat with red, white, and blue arrowhead canes within garlands of canes surrounding central cluster with shamrock motif, all set in white latticinio. $3\frac{1}{4}$″ diameter. *Circa* 1845–60

42

Antique Baccarat white star-dust carpet with silhouette canes of animals, birds, butterfly, and flower, dated B 1848. 3″ diameter. *Circa* 1845–60

Antique Baccarat sulphide of huntsman and dog set in translucent green ground. Top printy and facet cutting. 3″ diameter. *Circa* 1845–60

Antique Baccarat butterfly within circle of canes. Deep star cutting across base. 3″ diameter. *Circa* 1845–60

Antique Baccarat strawberries, foliage, and stalk. Star cutting on base. 3″ diameter. *Circa* 1845–60

Modern Baccarat canes set in white latticinio. 3″ diameter. Undated

Modern Baccarat close millefiori with zodiacal silhouettes and date 1969. 3″ diameter

Modern Baccarat with central silhouette of squirrel surrounded by circles of canes – one of silhouettes of different animals and birds, all set in white latticinio. Dated on base 1972. 3″ diameter

Clichy

CLICHY was the third factory to specialize in glass paperweights. Founded by Joseph Maës, the first glassworks was situated at Billancourt (Sèvres) in 1837, a year or so later moving to Clichy-la-Garenne, a suburb of Paris. As time went on, the quality of their products became increasingly higher and by the time of the Exposition in 1844 could be equated with the fine pieces made by Saint-Louis and Baccarat. In fact Clichy was awarded the top prize for excellence at this Exposition, and continued to win further prizes – for the clearness of its glass and for its coloured overlays – at international exhibitions.

In 1853 at the Crystal Palace Exhibition in New York, Clichy was awarded two medals for its exhibit, which included a variety of paperweights. They were the only glassworks to take part in the glass section of the Great Exhibition in London in 1862, later showing at the French Expositions of 1867 and 1878.

During the years 1846–52 many superb paperweights were made, quite different in variety and colouring from those made by Saint-Louis and Baccarat. The attractive swirl paperweights were made only by Clichy, as well as those with the moss ground. They excelled in their few flower and many colour grounds. The Clichy rose, in different colours, was a particularly attractive addition to their millefiori canes.

In 1885 the factory was bought by a family called Lander who had a glassworks at Sèvres. The company was then renamed *Cristalleries de Sèvres et Clichy*, but the quality of its products declined and the company soon ceased trading.

Antique Clichy bouquet of pansy, bud rose, bud, thistles, green foliage, and stalks tied with pink ribbon. 2¾″ diameter. *Circa* 1845–60

Antique Clichy with clusters of canes set in opaque green cushion. 3″ diameter. *Circa* 1845–60

48

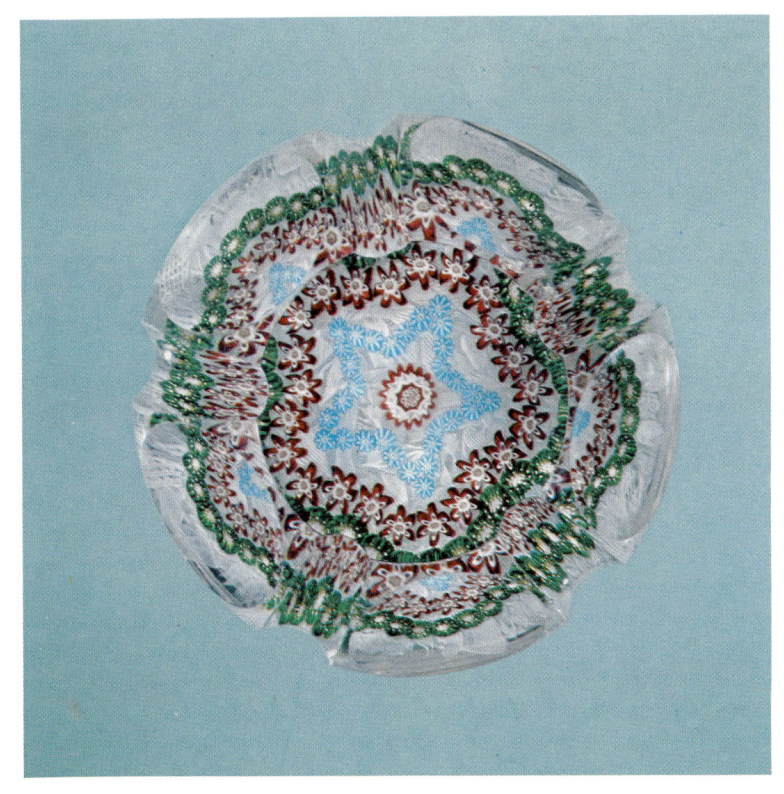

Antique Clichy star-shaped garlands of canes set in white latticinio. Cut with top and side printies, divided by flute cutting. 3″ diameter. *Circa* 1845–60

Antique Clichy concentric circles of canes, including white roses. 3¼″ diameter. *Circa* 1845–60

Antique Clichy blue and white double overlay with mushroom of concentric circles of canes and pink and white roses, contained in royal blue and white striped basket. Cut with top and side printies. Star cutting on base. 3″ diameter. *Circa* 1845–60

Unusual Clichy millefiori with central cluster of pink and white Clichy roses, all set in translucent red ground. 3″ diameter. *Circa* 1845–60

Clichy triple swirl. 3″ diameter. *Circa* 1845–60

51

The Gillinder Family

WILLIAM T GILLINDER was born in 1823 at Gateshead, near Newcastle upon Tyne, and spent the early part of his life in the Birmingham glass area. He started work in a glass house at the age of 8, and at 16 he was giving lectures in chemistry to his fellow workmen. At 20 he had an elegant shop.

In 1851 his talents were recognized when he was made Secretary of the National Flint Glass Makers Society of Great Britain and Ireland, a post he held for only two years because by then he had become an executive at the main shop of the New England Glass Company in Cambridge, Massachusetts.

Before William Gillinder left Birmingham he had made paperweights, learning the art at Bacchus and Sons. In New England he learned more about making paperweights from a Frenchman working there at the time.

After a brief time in New England he moved around the United States, finally owning his own factory, Gillinder & Sons in Philadelphia in 1861, where among other things he made moulded glass paperweights of different sorts, including one of Abraham Lincoln and George Washington, and various animal weights.

William Gillinder died in 1871, and his sons, James and Frederick, took over the business.

In 1912 James's three sons left Gillinder & Sons to found Gillinder Brothers at Port Jervis, New York. This Company is still in business but the Philadelphia factory closed in 1930.

Gillinder red and white double overlay with mushroom of concentric circles of canes set in white basket. Cut with top and side printies. Star cutting on base. $2\frac{3}{4}''$ diameter. *Circa* 1876

Gillinder. Colourless glass encloses figure of black horse resting on a white paper disk which is inserted in underside of weight. Horse's head and tail move. (There is also a turtle weight with moving head and legs.) $2\frac{1}{4}''$ diameter. *Circa* 1876

Paul Ysart and Family

PAUL YSART comes from a family of glass makers. His father, Salvadore, and grandfather, were glass blowers, as were his brothers Augustine and Vincent.

Paul was born in Barcelona in 1904, and in 1915 he came to Scotland with his father and brothers. His father joined the Edinburgh and Leith Flint Glass Company (now Edinburgh Crystal) in that year, and at the age of 11 Paul started his apprenticeship there with his brothers.

A year later the family moved to Glasgow, working at a glass factory named Cochrane which no longer exists. In the 1920s the Ysarts moved to Perth and worked with John Moncrieff. The main product of their efforts was a type of glass known as Monart, designed by Mrs Moncrieff but made only by the Ysarts. They probably made the odd paperweight too, but only those made by Paul achieved any real standard. In 1948 his father and two brothers left Moncrieff and started up their own business in a wooden shed in Perth. Paul never got on with his father who liked to maintain strict control over his family, so he remained with Moncrieff, making Monart glass and some of his best paperweights.

Paul's father and brothers worked until 1956 under the first name of Ysart Brothers, making inexpensive weights of not very high quality and coloured glass vases and bowls, sold under the name of Vasart. The father and Augustine both died in 1956 leaving the business in financial difficulties.

In 1963 Paul Ysart went to Wick to join Caithness Glass as Training Officer but continued to make paperweights, chiefly for the American market. In 1971 he left Caithness Glass to work on his own where he still makes fine paperweights signed 'PY' for collectors in America, and other fine unsigned weights for sale in Great Britain – mainly for the gift trade.

Modern Scottish butterfly within circle of canes set in smokey ground, by Paul Ysart. 2¾" diameter. Probably made in 1965

Modern Scottish bouquet of flowers, foliage, and stalks, within circle of canes set in smokey ground, incorporating signature cane PY, by Paul Ysart. 2¾" diameter. Probably made in 1965

Modern Scottish close millefiori cluster within circle of canes, by Paul Ysart. 2¾″ diameter. Probably made in 1965

Modern Scottish weight with cluster of canes set in smokey ground, by Paul Ysart. 2¾″ diameter. Probably made in 1965

56

The Story of Perthshire Paperweights

Vasart was temporarily given a new lease of life in 1956 with the introduction of outside help and some glass decorating work; and in 1960 Stuart Drysdale, a lawyer practising in the neighbouring town of Crieff, was invited to give it administrative support. The decorative work ceased, however, the output being confined to three basic paperweights and the Vasart vases. By this time the business was known as a limited company under the name of Vasart Glass. Various other contract work was sought, including the manufacture of light globes for the reconstructed Downing Street residence of the Prime Minister. In 1963 the business was on its feet, but only just, when the rapid expansion of one of their contracts called for a complete reconstruction.

A new factory was built at Crieff, trading under the name of The Strathearn Glass Company, and continued the old basic products. In 1967 the arrival of a copy of an American drug store magazine *Woman's Day* immediately alerted Stuart Drysdale and the craftsmen to the fact that the fine paperweights made in the nineteenth century put their own work to shame. Dissension on management policy led Stuart Drysdale to leave the firm and revert to his law practice, but a plea followed immediately from the craftsmen to start up again so that they could try to match their skills to those of the nineteenth-century workers at Saint-Louis, Clichy, and Baccarat factories.

An abandoned school building was rapidly found and rented at £100 per year; the necessary equipment to make a start was installed in three months; and Tony Moravec, a very experienced glass cutter, and one or two others, mostly raw apprentices, moved in to join Stuart Drysdale and get the operation started. They decided to call themselves Perthshire Paperweights Ltd.

It was not long before the firm's reputation started to grow and the school building, which had only been regarded as temporary, was soon too small, so a small modern factory was built and equipped on the Muthill Road to the south of Crieff. The factory has now grown, employing some 25 people from this small town, most of them very young and possibly not fully aware of the great impression they are making.

Each year collectors are able to buy limited editions of paperweights of great variety, which in time will become investments as new collectors seek the previous editions now 'out of print'. Paperweights unlimited in number are also produced very reasonably priced, and increasingly popular with people looking for unusual and attractive gifts.

Modern Perthshire dahlia-head, cut with top and side printies. 3″ diameter. Made in 1972

Modern Perthshire dragonfly within circle of canes. 2½" diameter. Made in 1970

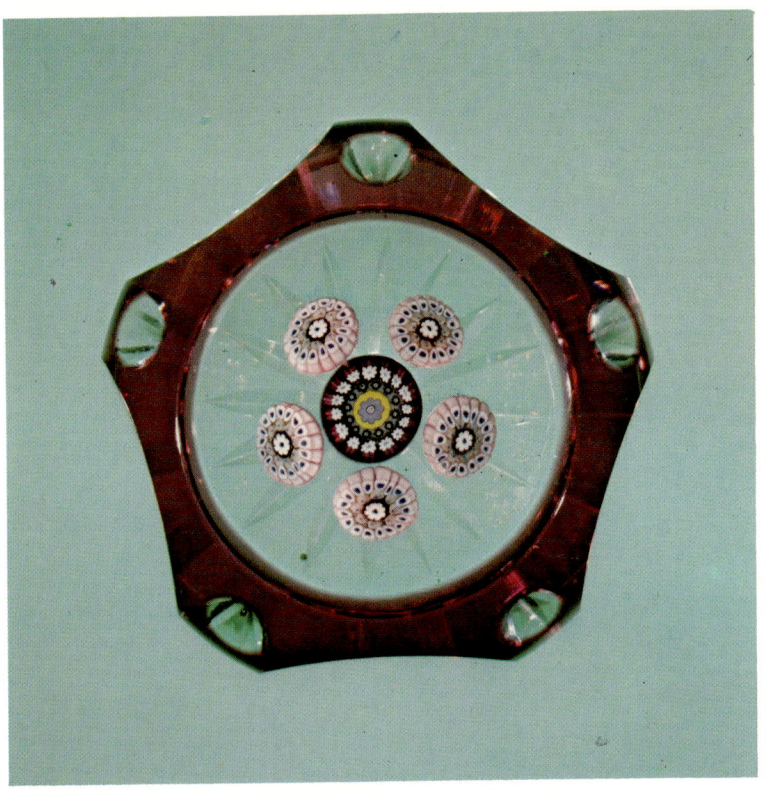

Modern Perthshire translucent red flash overlay with cluster of canes within. Cut with top and side printies. Star cutting on base. 3" diameter. Made in 1970

Modern Perthshire with pattern of canes and white filigree set in opaque green cushion. 3″ diameter. Made in 1971

Modern Perthshire animal silhouette canes, and date P 1973, set in carpet of rods and above translucent amethyst base. Cut with top and side printies. 2½″ diameter

60

Modern Perthshire Christmas 1972 weight with mistletoe within circle of canes set in red cushion. $2\frac{1}{2}''$ diameter

Modern Perthshire pattern of canes set in red cushion. Date cane in base P 1974. 3″ diameter

Modern Perthshire flower with signature P in centre, foliage, and stalk. Cut with top and side printies. Strawberry cutting on base. Miniature size, 2″ diameter

Modern Perthshire white clematis, buds, foliage, stalks, and signature P cane, set in mauve cushion. 3″ diameter

Modern Perthshire purple and white double overlay with close millefiori cushion within, dated P 1974. 2¾" diameter

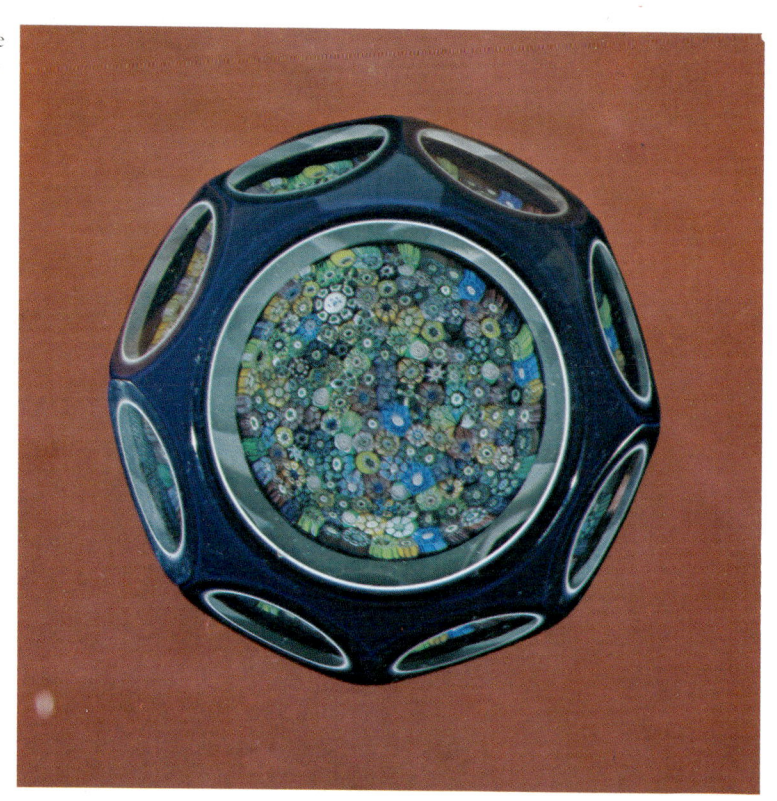

Modern Perthshire bouquet of pansy and clematis, foliage, and stalks tied with ribbon bow, with hovering dragonfly. Cut with top and side printies. Strawberry cutting on base. Signature P in cane in centre of pansy. 3¼" diameter

Oriental Paperweights

During this century the Chinese and Japanese, with their great skill as copiers, have produced colourful and sometimes pretty weights. Only three examples are included in this book but give some idea of the small ones made. Others, large and small, have delicate water lily-type flowers in pink and white, some having the attractive feature of a tiny green frog sitting on a leaf. They can mostly be found in a market or gift shop at very little cost, from about 50p to £1, although a particularly attractive weight was sold by auction in London for £35. The unusual and delicate weight illustrated, larger in size, containing a very fine imitation of a white Amaryllis with yellow stamens, was sold by auction for £42. If they are well made and attractive, therefore, they can hold their own amongst other modern paperweights in a collection.

The glass has an oily texture, and is lighter in weight, making the paperweights easily identifiable against the finer crystal of the antique and some other modern weights.

Modern Chinese with upstanding coloured arum-type lilies. Miniature size, 2″ diameter

Modern Chinese pink water lily and foliage. Miniature size, 2″ diameter

Chinese white Amaryllis set in clear glass. 3″ diameter

Museums with Glass Paperweights

GREAT BRITAIN

Birmingham City Art Gallery and Museum, Birmingham.
Glynn Vivian Art Gallery, Swansea, Wales.
Victoria and Albert Museum, London.
Museum and Art Gallery, Bristol.

CONTINENT

Conservatoire National des Arts et Métiers, Paris.
Cristalleries de Saint-Louis, Paris.
Cristalleries de Baccarat, Paris.
Musée des Arts Décoratifs, Louvre, Paris.
Musée du Verre, Liège, Belgium.

UNITED STATES OF AMERICA

Bergstrom Art Center and Museum, Neenah, Wisconsin.
The Art Institute of Chicago.
Bennington Museum, Bennington, Vermont.
Brooklyn Museum, Brooklyn, New York.
Corning Museum of Glass, Corning, New York.
The Chrystler Art Museum, Provincetown, Massachusetts.
M. H. de Young Museum, San Francisco.
Edward L. Doheny Memorial Library, Camarillo, California.
St. Mary's Seminary, Perryville, Missouri.
Henry Ford Museum, Dearborn, Michigan.
New York Historical Society, New York City.
Old Sturbridge Village, Sturbridge, Massachusetts.
Sandwich Historical Society Museum, Sandwich, Massachusetts.
Smithsonian Institution, Washington D.C.
Peterborough Museum, Peterborough, New Hampshire.
Toledo Museum of Art, Toledo, Ohio.
Illinois State Museum, Springfield, Illinois.

Bibliography

BEDFORD, JOHN *Paperweights* New York: Walker and Company, 1968.

BERGSTROM, EVANGELINE H. *Old Glass Paperweights* Chicago: The Lakeside Press, 1940. New York: Crown Publishers, Inc., 1947.

CLOAK, EVELYN CAMPBELL *Glass Paperweights of the Bergstrom Art Center* New York: Crown Publishers Inc., 1969.

ELVILLE, E. M. *Paperweights and Other Glass Curiosities* London: Country Life Ltd., 1954.

HOLLISTER, PAUL Jr. *The Encyclopedia of Glass Paperweights* New York: Clarkson N. Potter, Inc., 1969.

HOLLISTER, PAUL Jr., and LANMON, DWIGHT *Paperweights: Flowers which Clothe the Meadows* New York: The Corning Museum of Glass, Corning, New York, 1978.

IMBERT, R., and AMIC, Y. *Les Presse-Papiers Français* Paris: Art et Industrie, 1948.

JOKELSON, PAUL *Antique French Paperweights* Privately published, 1955. *One Hundred of the Most Important Paperweights* Privately published, 1966. *Sulphides* New York: Thomas A. Nelson, 1968.

McCAWLEY, PATRICIA K. *Antique Glass Paperweights from France* London: Spink & Son Ltd., 1968.

MACKAY, JAMES A. *Glass Paperweights* London: Ward Lock Limited.

MANHEIM, FRANK J. *A Garland of Weights* New York: Farrar, Straus & Giroux, 1967.

MELVIN, JEAN SUTHERLAND *American Glass Paperweights and Their Makers* New York: Thomas A. Nelson, 1967.

STANKARD, PAUL *Flora in Glass* London: Spink & Son Ltd., 1981.